Meet the GREEN BAY PACKERS

PERCY LEED

Lerner Publications ◆ Minneapolis

Copyright © 2026 by Lerner Publishing Group, Inc.

Stats in this book are accurate through the 2024 National Football League season.

All rights reserved. International copyright secured. No part of this book may be reproduced, stored in a retrieval system, or transmitted in any form or by any means—electronic, mechanical, photocopying, recording, or otherwise—without the prior written permission of Lerner Publishing Group, Inc., except for the inclusion of brief quotations in an acknowledged review.

Lerner Publications Company
An imprint of Lerner Publishing Group, Inc.
241 First Avenue North
Minneapolis, MN 55401 USA

For reading levels and more information, look up this title at www.lernerbooks.com.

Main body text set in ITC Avant Garde Gothic Std.
Typeface provided by Adobe Systems.

Editor: Annie Zheng **Designer:** Mary Ross **Photo Editor:** Elena Mai

Library of Congress Cataloging-in-Publication Data

Names: Leed, Percy, 1968- author.
Title: Meet the Green Bay Packers / Percy Leed.
Description: Minneapolis : Lerner Publications, 2026. | Series: Lerner sports rookie. Terrific teams | Includes bibliographical references and index. | Audience: Ages 5–8 | Audience: Grades K–1 | Summary: "The Green Bay Packers won the first Super Bowl in NFL history. Discover more about the team's best players, greatest moments, thrilling stats, and more in this fun, high-interest book"— Provided by publisher.
Identifiers: LCCN 2024039762 (print) | LCCN 2024039763 (ebook) | ISBN 9798765668436 (library binding) | ISBN 9798765683668 (paperback) | ISBN 9798765681770 (epub)
Subjects: LCSH: Green Bay Packers (Football team)—History—Juvenile literature.
Classification: LCC GV956.G7 L44 2026 (print) | LCC GV956.G7 (ebook) | DDC 796.332/640977561—dc23/eng/20240829

LC record available at https://lccn.loc.gov/2024039762
LC ebook record available at https://lccn.loc.gov/2024039763

Manufactured in the United States of America
1-1011738-53811-2/25/2025

Photo Acknowledgments
Sports Studio Photos/Getty Images, p. 5; Tom Hauck/Getty Images, p. 7; Jamie Squire/Getty Images, p. 9; Cooper Neill/Getty Images, p. 11; John D. Hanlon/Sports Illustrated via Getty Images, p. 13; Focus on Sport/Getty Images, p. 14; Patrick McDermott/Getty Images, p. 17; Kevin C. Cox/Getty Images, p. 19; Stacy Revere/Getty Images, p. 21; AP Photo/Matt Ludtke, p. 22; Brooke Sutton/Getty Images, p. 23. Design elements: Kwangmoozaa/Getty Images; Andrii Shelenkov/Getty Images; AnthiaCumming/Getty Images.
Cover: Brooke Sutton via AP.

Table of Contents

Chapter 1 Green and Gold 4

Chapter 2 Big Moments 8

Chapter 3 Best Players 12

Chapter 4 Leading the Pack 18

Green Bay Packers Team Leaders 23

Glossary 24

Learn More 24

Index 24

★ CHAPTER 1 ★

Green and Gold

Quarterback Jordan Love threw the ball. His teammate Jayden Reed caught the pass in the end zone. Touchdown!

The Green Bay Packers joined the NFL in 1921.

The Packers are the third-oldest team in the league.

Lambeau Field

Until 1956, the Packers played their home games in Old City Stadium. They moved to Lambeau Field in 1957.

CHAPTER 2
Big Moments

In 1967, the Packers played in the first Super Bowl. They crushed the Kansas City Chiefs 35-10.

The 2011 Super Bowl was a close game. The Packers beat the Pittsburgh Steelers 31–25.

In the 2016 playoffs, the Packers scored in the last second. They beat the Dallas Cowboys 34–31.

In 2024, the Packers played the Cowboys in the playoffs again. The Packers won 48–32.

Best Players

Ray Nitschke kept the Packers defense sharp. He helped the team win two Super Bowls.

Forrest Gregg blocked for the Packers in the 1960s. He played in 188 straight games.

Running back and kicker Paul Hornung scored 62 touchdowns in nine seasons.

LeRoy Butler was a tough defender. He went to the Pro Bowl four times.

Brett Favre is one of the best quarterbacks of all time. He won three NFL MVP awards.

Aaron Rodgers took over as quarterback when Favre left. Rodgers led the Packers to a big win at the 2011 Super Bowl.

CHAPTER 4
Leading the Pack

The Packers are one of the most successful teams in the NFL.

They have won four Super Bowls. Only four teams have won more.

In 2021, the team added quarterback Jordan Love.

Running back Josh Jacobs joined in 2024.

The team has high hopes for these players. Fans can't wait to see where the Packers go next.

GREEN BAY PACKERS TEAM LEADERS

Passing touchdowns: Aaron Rodgers, 475
Passing yards: Brett Favre, 61,655
Receiving touchdowns: Don Hutson, 99
Rushing yards: Ahman Green, 8,322
Rushing touchdowns: Jim Taylor, 81

Glossary

end zone: the area at each end of a football field where players score touchdowns

MVP: Most Valuable Player

NFL: National Football League

Pro Bowl: the NFL's all-star game

Learn More

Downs, Kieran. *Football*. Minneapolis: Bellwether Media, 2024.

Flynn, Brendan. *Football*. Minneapolis: Early Encyclopedias, 2024.

Leed, Percy. *Football's Super Bowl*. Minneapolis: Lerner Publications, 2025.

Index

Love, Jordan, 4, 20

playoffs, 10–11

Pro Bowl, 15

Super Bowl, 8–9, 12, 17, 19

touchdown, 4, 14